SKIN OF NOCTURNAL APPLE

Misha Honcharenko

Translated from the Ukrainian
by the author

with an afterword by
Nick Blackburn

Pilot Press
London

For my mother

"DIFFERENCE"

Do you hear? As if through stretched out his arms and upward
because she intertwined
As never before, holding the tree crowns
Communication. Look in and wake up
Oh, I'm still here grinning give attention to the glances next to
the silence is wild laughter
Shiver - why?

20.03.2018

Cutting the lines
The water whirlwind is raging
I rise
And as if in a trance
I start
R
T
To cope with
Danc-
Ing
Dark red lights
Dipped me in color
Don't let me be you
Because you are my catharsis
mon lamentation
smells fragrant
Warm shadows are circling
Come here
Round and beautiful
Thy cheeks
Washes me
This shapeless liquid

24.03.2018

overcoming drops
and twice hands
pulse and nerve
squinting eyes
after all
the great depths of space fetter
and love me laughing
wildly jerome
no laugh chameleon
Leia so impeccable
I can and so transparent
in delicate shells of different manifestations
blue and gray do not hold on
to plump legs and breathe
like a fish in water

29.03.2018

"BEATRICE"

Be truthful
Among the pupils
of someone's eyes
Blackish and red
In compressed form
Glorious and young
Exclaim and Contemplate
Slowly Mornings and
Trees are Thickened
Velour And striped
Black coat And saying
White noises
Disappeared and
Hole swallowed up your
Population like black and white
Triptych
Create with craziness
Compulses foid
Sneak and whisper
your machinery comme mon

30.03.2018

Persival
And the water grumbles through him
I need a night light I revel in
Fearless despondency and the sweet
Taste of lime.
Transparent castle wall
White towels of pictures
You abound in an hour and a spear
The wall was torn and was painted with oil.
Lawns and warm waters
Pebbles and camp.
Plunging your head into the water
You remember the smiling nostalgia.

08.04.2018

Wall and coming
Wet fibers fall rather
Metaphorically.
And you smell like the Gentle breeze of Magonia,
The rock turned around
My gene mutations
Winter light
And I see you again
Windows are fearfully breaking
Making everyone fear and what else
Field of vision gaze
My eye is enclosed
And convulsions seem to be Some act
Parfaite.
Not enough
Gunpowder and fright
His pale cheekbones.
Radically I am never waiting for you.
Hope.

20.04.2018

"YOU WERE NEVER THERE"

Remember when you were there?
Imperceptibly, like a chameleon
Having said a word, breathing
More and more
Fingers went numb, do you even remember?
Convulsions, dress and - You are domineering, and I ask
About the structure of consciousness
Keeping with you a
Piece of memory
Clanging with the crow's fingers and my death - is all this
necessary?
I do not care, grain and blurry I tear the wall, and you and
Nothing, no, it was not.

18.05.2018

now hold on bow command
laughing dropping a chair a knife plunging into me
with my petit models le fountain you through me
small convolutions of your lips rustle pierce
caress my transparent smoldering bowl
with a rotating dome
darky squirrels I mopped them
with a baroque rococo mop

13.06.2018

the diaphragms twisted into a simple one
Insolence left floating past the past
Analysis point equals uncertainty
Mind throwing back, drowning it out with glass
Your pattern went into an open wound
Murder is not enough to bury this matter
Spiral reduced your movement
For each of my positions
Spiritual roast killed everything in me
Smoke and gourmet crooked living
Harmonization sealing
Recent creepy smart and scarce
Sediment came to us
Perceived died and left
Your sharp and unfinished Paradise.

16.06.2018

"... DID YOU DESTROY?"

steam electrophoresis streets
east and reality
clove and unrealistic
double transparent
with a stern look arisen
uneven use of shit your fading is gone
the pump absorbs
the refectory rejoices
sour quirks from the script
gone and did not recognize
turn into something watery and
from memory dominates
hypertrophied thin and mesh
zealous, ardent and carousel horror
bold letters and light handwriting of
your letter Left me in a light bulb
making me feel choking.

23.06.2018

"WET CURTAINS"

The most ancient way
The lot is death
To kill to love to burn
Predictions soar and will not
Fold all the puzzles inside
Pandora's box the world is open
All illusion and fear
Transparent flasks inside the nerve
Nerve inside everything and
There was no desire to kill
Power the reason is this
Electronic owner crumbled To dust and panics
Time drips and grumbles looks deadly

25.06.2018

Wet smooth surface erases
Feminine look unique
Wet shine of your tears rustles
Abnormal and immoral
Hills of ethical norms carefully
But leave without fear
Dropping flannel strips
The noise of your pain dies and resurrects
Too simple and painful
It would seem to accept and fix your gaze
But everything is not so
The forest absorbed and protected with moisture
Killed and resurrected
All voices repeat: The dark color of joy

09.07.2018

Do not hold my
Lame I slipped out
My noble drop
Brushwood stumbled
Intersecting emotions through hands
Rhythm felt through the film
Only your stubborn ones with holes
Forced: to scent
Peace through glass
And against the background of your bokeh the
Color is so brighter, the wholeness is better
Cool yellow

10.07.2018

"FORGOTTEN MINE AND MY EYES"

Sleepy streets of the eyes are light repetitive and the air is
uneven pushed large and hated
Candles burn incessantly and a red square in the name of the
flame enters
Lines of the heart in the mind Lavender smack of bitterness
rustles and grumbles
The survivor is coming and demands
Words about the eyes that flood us, whole pain wrapped around
your hungry gaze
 Your developing hair and your only smile
That will remain inside my ball with memorias lonely
cheekbones fastened tore out femininity
There is only a mirror of your eyes and I look and enter the
abyss.

17.07.2018

"BLACK SPOT AROUND"

You will come and the voice will sound
Indeed the nerve sounds loudly
The inner zeal of the fragments
Come to nothing and walk freely for yourself
The grateful shade of your smile
A weak languid voice chops
The favorite of fatigue of the smell
The decay of you and the center of the abyss stared and
cautiously said: would you please steal your body?
My body is inside the epicenter
Soul will not allow to leave without an answer
High but central
Electricity of the voice after
Screams tears and screams
Who fucking cares?

24.07.2018

Without releasing the tulip from
Under my crazy branches, make me: turn
Speech and steel
Pay attention to the long and
Unchanging humming noise
From your box it brings
Shivering through the bodies of people
Milk from under the bark Is dead that is stoic
Eureka body movement
Along my path to lies
We absorb and create
Smells of smoke from cigarettes and
Salt, sugar and honey
Front-line and impeccable
Platoon of circus society
Take mistrustful, take contemptuous supervision
My body is indestructible.

29.07.2018

Cold new people
Fell asleep in closed vacuums
Torturing broken norms
Small footprints outside the city
I'm blissfully looking around
On my hand the lines are torn apart by
Rays of darkness outside the heart
Face in the shadow and righteous
I burn my ears impossible
I lick the picture inside
My mind your
Arrow could have hit but did not hit
and spread your scent
Passionately desired and blessed

06.08.2018

Dark summer fire
Bridled the people at the foot
They said rejoice the fibers
Strengthened and loved the drive
The music of your sob moan
You look in the glass and lick the wounds
of foreign tribes and the color of your eyes
Punk grows in all yours
Run and be something worthy
The simple story of your voice and the
Silky Soprano

26.08.2018

you sit in zero gravity, the wet cold zinc galvanizes and gives the tree a juicy shade of pranks grateful for the crown of pity and rage respect what the holy fool is good for dying must be so nice york empty area alternate and stand in line yourself creature kisses possessing truth useless objects after the fire cutesy and non-trivial plastics snort tearing apart the ethics of the human patient dressing the word ugly and no family art with blood the owner painted modern you are already and interesting one on the other side wanderers killed do not look there central call him and there is no truth god heat cold disgust of the body the state is indistinct and we lived like this and we will live on simple problems were reputed and drowned in the ocean of our paradise boasting strike smoke and people society dust bullets screaming brushwood stone road whispered mentally fuck it

27.08.2018

glass ears dissecting the cavity the owner of the rectangular life-
giving one grabbing the handle and looking out the door fearing
panic about the horror no more furious roar from her body came
and pulsed I stand with my head buried and waiting for the
culmination, slowly looking and obliviously later, with my eyes
closed, the property has gone very far palace dinner ohoho gossip
kick under the table contempt humiliation bashful and cynical
eyes seem to bite into flesh and madly want at the same time

06.09.2018

wax coming from outside
mahogany owns stale
street of disease eminent
prison of roses fight power
revolution of mind
gentle streets of sex temptation
wet path of love and cold apple flavor of passion
pencil and soul outlines
elastic silky ecstasy
uneven main pain only center your face
decorated with your favorite sepia noises
removed only retro hairs cover
naked bodies human clear
frequent voices vibrate
I am unconscious remember my hands
and smile at the sight

31.08.2018

light cloudy twilight
the airy smell of love
conceals an irrational subtext
to eat and pull off the skin of distrust
push of a cubist masochist
creepy fight through sex
index of your bosom steaming
consumable smell of earth
simulacra and mirror smoke
crunching bones to a drumbeat
cheap cigarettes smacking and inhaling
the memory of your painful steal
capillaries and eclipse fill moisture
existential decoration trees scene
midnight in the center of namelessness

08.09.2018

rectangular cold worker
road murder lantern
red whim bubble little thing
pot-bellied cubic sector algorithms
seventy-eight clicks
nose colorless and
neck color fragrance familiarity
is not slavery orgy tickles splashes

11.09.2018

lie down don't move
(turn away)
it's cold here, regrettably gentle gravity, wait
(no one will be)
head nods mercilessly speed fierce people will not understand
the law is not uniform
(like everything in this world)
the delicious sweetness of your mind the blue reflections of your
carpet rose in the air
(inside out)
take care of yourself, you are in my memory a berry that
envelops your body
(and heart)

18.09.2018

the echelon demanded about
us kissing towards an unknown person
formally outlined a map of the world
with her fingers on her body
chronos does not ask
dangerous background
transparent pearl perfume line reflection
mirror hair red
you are beautiful to touch me and you other skin
but you are alone and your replica is in my ears
you are alone
are you mad?
take off your hat of senses
have some tea
no
better just shut up.

19.09.2018

to paint with gestures to own signals
spreading on the water your profile
excites and my desire is great to
collect a picture from your life
to live dim light comes from outside
the smell of lavender my corpse
is yours and the ladder of prospects
of desires with my hands
I hold a brush hate the face does not give out
the tree of life inside you burns
the language in me and
you are like an ascetic calling

24.09.2018

a woman with a stroller and a dog
an elderly woman old soviet union
en moi bicycle and an old man
a holy fool flowers and the smell of a burning body
a box without love and inside no one
engraving is beautiful painful
no need to twitch moving to pain
dancing child without a single sign
lively and emotional fractures
secretly concluding the act of the moment
his head in my direction ombre he is squared
and the clothes turned into
a kind of transparent asphalt and asphalt
at the feet and summer you know
quite for yourself

28.09.2018

pass the lollipop sweet tongue
combing your leg and
smiling opening the windows
I give you a smile of people
walk rush hour music and your thorny paths
through the crowd unbuttoning your trenchcoat
revealing your scarf reveling in a shower
as cold as your coffee and pretending
that you are absurdly not scary not feasible courtyard
your dark voice was receding to blame for that my eye
captivated you by the patterned view of your room
a gloomy shade added paint machine mechanisms
all extract current
and charge of the unknown
I lead my hand behind my coat good
you don't want to be touched and killed hope for bliss
move inside yourself to see in me a movie
your precious treasure

29.09.2018

Embracing conventionally (pulling out of) youth
until we need a celebration of adoration of a pill and should
enveloping hair the beauty of you
and the ice flows down the triangle of shadows of power
squeezing against the tree foreign nonresidents
will lie younger but my beloved is not worse than no I catch it
caressing my lips possessing and hiding strong alcohol on the
table why not play an intermediate moment
the body is alive in me and the whim of the buttocks and nipples
in the world please do not let go

03.10.2018

verbal one and two shadows than where and generally sweeter
turnover section what does the line refer to

priestesses grow and germinate near the gray and wet bushes
singing: wonderfully my hands are intertwined and unity

let me transform the mask and never wear it, I call this sim life
sea ferry pilgrim card with me and I create.

eagerly knowledge about everything intimacy frankly dark
and secretive

03.10.2018

looks sourly at himself
sees the body straightened
but I do not see myself
eyes are covered with a
cornice wrapped fraught with
saliva in illness and fear on my shoulder
I lie and think what
kingdom is your pain licking nipples and circles
I take off a mole around like a film
and I merge them inside you like an abyss
in a fairy tale the tongue inside the womb vibrates with a moan
and hide my true apple-colored buttocks and your
penis swollen over me
the gloomy interior added fire into the bright
range of terrible passion, are you even mine?

05.10.2018

hold carry away run away in the water
I hold my hand and the honey smell of my shoulders unfolds me
I will live inside a den called the larynx
going down the path and not fall hard and hard arteries
I cling and you greedily let me go separately you put me to sleep
and hugging my naked body you want about love you have not
heard

worshiping someone who knows no one I lose the thread from
the connection a torn jacket and I pulled out my teeth and my
mind hiding in the field it will find the unknown and moreover
my half in the sphere and in the river I am swimming and in the
water nowhere and no one to be yourself and nature together
running to nowhere.

milk shocks of water a wave-like vase went my cry
inside be a part of their act he is in warm cuts fresh your
emotions

06.10.2018

a face that is unique and tasteful of salt red sweater
removed lived rotted away
the attic of shelters of the sound of death
eyebrow petals scattered
I turn on the music inside the sad wing of a lost boy
who skillfully fought on the core a field
of the smell of love and memory on
which the light stands swearing and do not return

06.10.2018

I will cut it down, I will start chasing the windows
the mirrors moisture dumb to live
you are afraid but you don't want a house
blackness and hunger prowling prey hidden
but I cease to be surprised at the mind of people one beats
myself a table broken
the second masturbated to his feet in space
dances walk to let me into their shells no thanks
I'd rather be madness your nightmare

06.10.2018

fluctuations under the discharge of lies I'm a traitor
a deceiver down there
I'm sitting smiling
if you only knew how
having thrust a funny grin into the sea
the whale is strangling the fish inside and will not work out
and it's hard not to get patronage out there where it is a
no.

07.10.2018

articulation my country verbiage
distant with my back laying my head
was not waiting for my not bilious
dry law not an idea I merge with a lonely point
to save black turns at the price
spraying sessions of the patient imagination
instead of wine language is sweeter more yes

12.10.2018

i am kind of indecisive
way pronounced as
no deeper than you
immerse consume
helmet full of
oblivion smelling
swear not to be a
wayfarer
jagged mountains
and i'm burning
laving dropping
slaves under
queue bursting
flamed me up
rolling my body
up and down
satisfied?

14.10.2018

with an oily finger
the gloom of the double-wandering purple
forgot the hair
the road rustles with his eyes
freely painfully frankly a shadow
casting a triumph at the edge of the eye socket
will wipe take it away take it away proud lunar
where can you stop sharpening the point is it prudent
through coordination I can hardly remember
hiding at the root

21.10.2018

I'm in the center of a strange raw eating
he squeals and smells the skin
melting the house a relative wandering along the samples
broken walked along tiles slain flora you everywhere I
see a door there a child in a painting
revived and emerged with lips trembling fingers
the inscription transform building extraneous squeaks
of stilts in acid dissolved nerves
other thin hungry

24.10.2018

greedy face disgustingly coldly
bravissimo independently lays down
a wet head covered with pearls
than the period of euphemisms broadcasting
and shamelessly begging was completely
disappeared in the cage more tender
and stronger than the spiritual and blissful

03.11.2018

I cover my eyes with mold
I clog my mouth with moss
I'm sorry I'm looking after I'm emaciated
praying the error and sinfulness of human creature twirls skin
suffers a black stream of memorable noble
and independent snow-white on the equator destruction by mud
getting closer to the bowl of pacification
and weakness pressing shouting
she sang almost without noise and
penetrated
opened
everything that could be opened

04.11.2018

vulnerability straight off
face abandoned
outlines of bile
bleach underground
with saliva sticky tape
deep brothel with
narrow mind broadening
rotten my disciple within
disdain tighten bones
you wanted me with
my tongue being pleased

15.11.2018

tremendous leaping out
swirling unmade position
pondering awoken inside
severed hellish disaster
muttering twirling mah
wanted some milk of
whaur dae ye pleading
am tint catharsis
pimping sluggish noble
triplet poor spilled
dinnae feart ain yer
madden vandal barbaric

18.11.2018

the trickster jumps under the bright fading of the form moisture near it is more difficult to sit in a plate saucer tears crackles with a tea twist sacred possessions plastic dance portrait foil pale brown furniture crimson curtains blanket in color bells and magazine signal the crumpled world of writing give rise to whims situational love coffee wine stronger much stronger spill on me is a white gray table mirrored windows shower not dank to fragile street cigarette butts and no sweetness.

30.11.2018

dense covers the ground
with a cloth kissed with lace and floral blue
and forgetting about the slightly open window
brownish shadows on her face with grace
washes the fountain of cuts at the foot of the ribs
and you descend into whim barely coloring the clearing with
constellations on the breasts
retaining sprinkling with lavender
and absorbs sucks narrowly wide

11.12.2018

the blinding out-of-bounds
big difference in the hidden shades of transparent
une chair rips off the creatures' veils
landscape irrational of you are yours
my draw dictionary clippings gluing me
together I will make an object and you will decorate
embellishments with sparkling lines and lightning
splashing sauce and 4: 3
flying black lines yes you are a movie and
I am a visual stream yes I see humiliated
insulted and you 16: 9 negatives and you are
valuable beautiful film

12.20.2018

mimosas piled in a heap in sandy rows weakness
puddle minors in the center of a metropolis in you
anxiously inconsistency without limit and morals
weakness immoral poking at prayers rearrangement of
squealing need I will tie my soul closely I will look closely at the
epidermis and weakly
humming pleasing our voyeurs
with short people anxious without even trying to sigh

23.12.2018

smooth oval faces spoke the language
older than the place of transport at an angle
to the channel of prolonged laughter

02.01.2019

the blind side of the eye
sockets I wind circles up and down there
I'm not going to be a
Frenchman for a long time
and screaming with the utterly correct accent
je t'emmerde
median and bare nerves and pipes
brains raised eyelid another
dose of euphemisms

04.01.2019

there are future breakers and
having emerged into the gloomy one
that there is no need to kick
you said what will happen and
there is a smack of pain under the tongue
having tasted the same flesh
my dear callous milk man and everyone a millimeter of clothes
in burning and dying complaints look
my bag is collected in it I will find a mirror
my faint memories of the stench cracked
but not burnt ash still revolves
will remain in these hands and my smell will be

10.01.2019

where what
like me a false confession
the winding slopes of the hand of the eyes
I will hide my legs on my shoulder
ears near the body
I listen to the music of rumbling and shudder of sex in me

16.01.2019

the door muffles the smells of the eyes
gutted the faint moans of the fashionista
the hand is not the sea I am trying to understand
such that sharpness I cannot I can not fucking move
away gives as sharp as his knife persuades in captivity by the
refrigerator I answer my
your mother's father your boss
poet friend power
member of the union of the dismemberment
dividing sciences of art as you called
them now language trying
to drain blood into me?

19.01.2019

I evaporate with glass cold I
clean up with an apple peel
I pick up glorious gifts with water
I wash myself greedily with my teeth
I pronounce my aim and behold
your anatomical anonymous sandy
parts allegorically categorically
obliviously moving touching the body of the taste of sweetness
with the sea wave
the pier arising from the dream of
Morpheus trembles Dionysus

27.01.2019

if there was no whimsy
with a low unchanging desire
to be or to burn in a flame, heading:
here I am fettered by the changeable I will press
my elbows and fill with moisture with
my lower lip

06.02.2019

a block of stone with the smell of red hands
and fluent inferences with a healthy disposition I arrive gently
lapping a joyful willow with a train wrapped in pathetic
if you want you will not be glorious previous and bowing

26.02.2019

I see sections of leg stabs opening my
mouth saber-toothed transplant minute alarm two
I suck that moisture I bite off anger I masturbate and spoke that
there is warmth no one people kissing twins
became outside stinking black fibrous enter place
of arrival and departure
it cannot be

26.02.2019

nails cracked on them drawings of cavemen's fate
oh no no no up down two directions are considering bowels
flaunting from pain power thanatos and
slight infringement of freedoms and
eros body mutilated / alive
think

26.02.2019

I slave the roof of mankind in a leather jacket without
breaking with salt sweet hands on me pomegranate juice
tastes like your flesh milk rivers pool i drown bottomless
eyes and glasses

21.03.2019

yellow maples will be blessed will keep the river flow I swim
will absorb the skin peach skin apple lips
the back was drawn by the architect was
and will remember the picture on the bridge
when you smiled and breathed that smell of roses and mine

24.03.2019

I am torn fabric
young thin arms plexus
head cut frontal
crack fatigue touch mores
nerves delight

04.10.2019

bending my knees people hear the whole smooth
touch of the slow call the creation of pain
these are the same

19.04.2019

I forgot the look inside the tree covers
the grinding scent of your body kissing
pleasure is only one you love
I won't remember the shadow in
your garden enjoyment

10.05.2019

deliberately young constellation
background corpse retribution
take away the hat impact
pleasure there is not there no crack
not a clatter not a person
not cold not fast but loved or
maybe a fortune to destroy and
kill loneliness moment

14.05.2019

sweet unreliable sugary juice flows
with veins and ripped off my teeth and will
taste like I loved
you clean lips in promenade and kissed by the sun
called and hid in body and mind I considered a bit of
sweat your tears weren't enough honey
kissed with your lips covered with goosebumps
you are my incomprehensible

19.05.2019

doña syracuse under the shelter salut jumping between the life
of a cafe cellophane industry shivering a shot on a body with a
ponytail and an immense look at hair with paving stones
movable saturn medallion tongue young kissing pattern of
vibration incomprehensible stone decayed lips of youth
withering ornament with saliva and foam gently smoothed the
black woody earth as feasible as terrible as loved

24.05.2019

street in milk
frozen lips
in the steaming haze

04.06.2019

in the air I saw lips a low voice
woven from the noises of bodily silvery
I swam in the sea and wait and will wait for you
my personal kerouac the blissful ballad you will sing about the
innocence of shameless hands
oh he kept humanely going to meet the crimson lines
on your hand and surrounded your neck with veins
gently kissing

05.06.2019

said avalanche to endure and only cave hair
to save the eroticism of indulgence
extreme nudity of humiliation of the flesh
the ruler lovely dirt in the heart I did with my teeth
I wore and wear those innate nipples torn off with
spots with a reward of color disappointment
frightened limited scope
sick all in my arms that smell intoxicates
screaming I wish and obey

06.06.2019

screaming joy with your hand
to hold your face a block under
the Bosnian bloody street smell the reign of time
to pacify sweets under cellophane
cover rotten minds fourth street number
four hundred and six I liked the other day
I didn't want to smoke inhale the ash
paving stones my feet walked over me

17.06.2019

and the air breathed citrus
asked for shadows salty straight lines
created cold greedy I never died so much

15.07.2019

yes .. yes no .. yes .. i live.
legacy key closed
grimace kicked
feel sorry for the inseparable
the cliff is cruel
shallow gorge of the heart
body corners more beautiful
and my dress was closed
face changed
back in blue hands
rouge penetrated
on me from myself
found in myself and did not
pulled out saved
let go licking
licking wounds

28.07.2019

those milky chapped hands
wanted to disturb my knowledge
i never wanted
younger minds weaved the promised garden
you hold the skin and squeeze
floor painting the whole story of pain
start me
and cried with oil and salt
flower fading of your memory
cold shuddering river
your lips resemble sweetness
while lying on the tile I always wanted to remember
you like that
so wet so light

28.07.2019

barren ray reflects
the stairs were washed in blood
herbal cast on fire
she's nothing in the skin
a stranger smell
box of lips kissed
only in the backyard
saw hands sticking
our damned land
mouth open letting in grief

03.08.2019

apricot field I lay
florally bowed
at your feet and those
cheeks
caressed his lips
rough and smooth
your belly on which
a whole spot of my love
you must know
always
you are the one
always i will
and I want

03.08.2019

look at an object from the side
he is not afraid of himself in himself
but also such a homage to the portrait of the artist in his youth
and flesh in color
as if he himself draws something in his head
which could never be visualized
body censorship

08.08.2019

how easy is it to tell you
all my desire to fall
draw a picture
I loved and felt sorry for your face
and forgive for ignorance
my subtle bodily
hand battles
hysterical weakness
my friend my support
I call you that
with footprints I show
me then and there
you nod with your hand
ultimate abode of the chapter
which will never be
kiss

18.08.2019

"EPIPHANY OF EERIE LIFE EXISTENCE"

self-loathing strategy up to me
fragility of stubborn trust
audacious misogyny
i could talk to your body
like for hours
errogant weirdness
cure for self-consciousness
potential of being hatred
slippery slope babe
literally the best you
and xerox of your
jaws contemplating
by so many people out there
they want know how it's like
to be such horrible
dismissed raspy junk
and kissing soul
devil outstanding
exaggeration
acknowledging
dazed

23.08.2019

breaking waves with stolen glasses I
caught tart touches in the guise of amazing
grief I am free to act and the desire
to take your words to taste and
not spit out but to love to absorb the scene of silk
an enlarged equipped claw of the notorious
ugly bile time for a person
to move inward

23.09.2019

blind skin of my young
pale cannot walking stranger
I've seen your blackish eyes
devouring my performance
pouring naked water onto
wrists closed by your tears
red lips coastline my feet
flickering blue souls
crying out the
best they could
fading hands
snuggled up against your
temple
seriously
shudder
blurring you
are quite tender

29.10.2019

"IN ANY DIRECTION"

on fiercely forgotten faces
thirst attracts you to the dangerous contemplation of the content
of your sweet human lips
and on the street there is a broken cedar horizontally rotated
range of shimmering flickering their
hair and body without clothes are cool
forget it but remember when a blue bed languidly stole radiation
to get into your words the smell of the letter
that I keep for my love with a hungry movement in the sobbing
feet on the ceiling I want to lie looking at how you didn't want
to just
leave

21.11.2019

I'm not sick
I've never been I did a good job and slowly froze on small
freshwater stabbing wastelands
imposed by the voids Indirectly guilty humanly on the ground
when I don't know fading at low frequencies my streets
the dust that took my desires a tragedy and she always said why
I want to touch it hurts to touch the salt
palely merge into the combination of my deceased head and life
how damn good and
you said it would be great was innovative
but no matter how I wanted to shine
in the name

24.01.2020

"INTERLUDE"

I on the surface are much closer to your transparent winding
lines of eyes with the corners of my lips I pronounced on the
body and wanted to beautifully splash myself on the level
higher

Act 1

a. this is reality not not not fiction I have seen love and want
always on my strange visions, dreams and even beauty yours is
already more important and I want to remember forever the
words of roses, beer, the smell of eyes, the premises of the
disease, about a smile understanding words breaking hearts
preparing for a kiss
on the trees a crimson touch on transparent films curbing closed
covered blurred liberated

Act 2

the taste of lemon on the cheeks kissed tear-stained on the legs
on the hands on the shoulders to lie

head in the oasis and in the dark. whispers and sighs

and me you we cape water on each of us we fill and I live and
you live even more

23.02.2020

I had a tilted snow
Upside down
Walking errogant
Everything quietly
Subliminal
Orchestra allowed
To slowly beat
Bite spit cum
I would never had
Without the line
The stroke of mine
Consciousness to
Cruel policy
Orchid finely stays
His voice trembling
Lovingly

I am trust and fuck
Nearby and love
Neverwhere
Softly kissing
The blood hormones
Voice voice voice
Butter on the plate
With lost sounds
Wounded koral
Nipples glowing
Understood
Torn with tornado
On the same love
Lately

19.03.2020

I've kinda contributed narrative
enigma life exchange
hollow slightly lover
lower I wanted to transparent
lavishly facing covering
joints of scare wrapped
in sugar

20.03.2020

"THE BURIAL OF EMOTIONS"

She was injected at the door under the zero sign
He didn't want to cry, only I wanted
Man under cockroach street
Milky ironic floral
In my land I always lay and gloomy
Kissed kissed and kissed tenderly
Your cold hands underground
I poured and closed like a curtain

T. trembled and screamed into humanity into the hands he
kissed of the noble stabbing eyes on the walls.
He was like that and froze he was he was not afraid he killed me
loved the onion rings at the edge of the plate on the plate he was
looking out for the past

Warm up my soul cold food me
his me her all soulless eyes teeth like warmth from the words of
hungry I was so embarrassed to eat myself he so wanted to
awaken by force she was completely a wall I said she was sick
she was destroyed I body she is not loved

a thin blade around her wet face, legs, hands, abdomen, her
epidermis, so shrunk her thoughts shrunk beautifully thinks but
I was afraid I am so much afraid I want to fucking die and they
are in large numbers I don't see I'm blind I only open my past
her past they are like her

crimson face humbly in the gloom ached for me for all of you
and us
pure blood penis vagina
devours erection in waves
here are the narcotic eruptions
seed cry high low our

26.05.2020

"BANSHEE"

A textured body (not) affectionate evil gnarled keeper
of the ultimate creation of small and large faces
dark rotation of fruit acid and roundness
deep lip lines eyes nipples navel cuticles and teeth I wanted
to love and not only they are like my holiness and conjugation
enigmatic caresses melancholy
killing carnage of words of mind bodies coldness of thought and
bark non-whole male brief sweat smells various serious
exclamations indecision
forgetfulness of life beauty beauties paint combinations of blue
pale young milk to love a mature beloved, do not forget about
the need for the existence of coldness of coldness
I need you.

21.06.2020

"AT THE WALLS OF UNTOUCHABLE DEBTORS, A KISS THAT WAS FORGOTTEN AT THE EDGE OF THE IRRATIONAL"

the king saw desired a pacified face, in fact, I am so simple
l'appel du vide call of emptiness to run around shrill show teeth
junior caretaker he forgot himself on his body he taught me to
close myself as a neighbor I would like to hear those blazing
unhealthy stole

in the sheltered wastelands with vanity, pity fiddles with black
broad ancient letters

the king forgot about tenderness and covered with abomination
every word from his lips every stolen word every ruined place
where I lived and as if this should teach me how to create my
own out of nothing

bienheureux mort shading on your small pictures I remember
how beautiful the music sounded on your scary strokes killed by
eros the paint of a human stomach and whom you did not forget
to kill love to reanimate

it would be good if it all ended, you always wished it was short
and clear, I know I don't know the blood clots squeezed and
didn't unclench and your strong voice seemed to evaporate in
my stomach

languid hair wriggled in the king's garbage and you are a
dictator bizarre face with a crooked face and abnormal control

I sucked the silky fabric silk wandered into consciousness it
forgot who I was not born and at all

la paix no no no

the caretaker tried to forget what he saw but I forgot to turn off
the button seriously let's it be an illusion

28.07.2020

staring peering praying hungry scream squinting my eyes froze
in the pitch darkness blind familiar hum sweetly cold to you

holding me by the door
pale dirty hands
you will be blessed
frankly speaking
faintly see you in
my careful
short stays

spider thrusts on the body
maybe it's true and I love
but I don't want to do it so hard
I apply the most gentle movements
these hands
truly you

largest swim
have you seen that freedom
salty breeze body hands
the movements of my mind and
weakness moans like
signals of my complete
full-fledged
real me

beauty is not enough
and your health
will not be enough

03.10.2020

"PENETRATION GENERATION"

unbearably painful
it hurts with blood
thanatos adorns the flesh
villages in roses with thorns
crying peacefully

my country is raped
those who themselves wanted love
attempt to justify
very good
Badly
and why
gently
rage flared
but i didn't try
cope with audio
groans of those grievances
whispers of the glorious
rapist
I look shrilly
screaming at the ceiling
evolution did not happen

take your blood away
to stay on your
body and life
meat

23.04.2021

cheerful fatigue
my voice am
makes you think about
the voice of
wandering with
hiding place
Understand
short words

20.06.2021

Afterword

The Nipple of the World

This is a collection about freedom, what else do you want to know?

That Ukraine is a free, sovereign state, and will survive us.

That this collection, which is free, opens four years and one month into the invasion of Ukraine on 20 February 2014 and moves beyond our seeing half a year or more before the initiation of war, 24 February 2022. It may be it is more the desire of my own nation that this threshold be disclosed here, a nation of flag-wavers, arms-dealers, life-fuckers. Skin stretches this far, and this far only.

That the nipple (buttocks and nipples, licking nipples and circles, those innate nipples, Nipples glowing) is sensitive, milk-bearing but does not rape. Ukraine is a country which knows about rape, where the earth remembers. This collection flowers within the soil which provides the world's grain, the soil where flowers the nipple of the world, which is the soil of an ongoing genocide. We will kill one million. We will kill five million. We will obliterate them all. We will drive the children into the raging river. We will throw the children into burning huts. They should not exist at all. We should execute them by firing squad. Ukraine, whose symbol is the sunflower, is free and will survive us.

This is a collection by one who knows tarot, in whose name I have drawn: the page of pentacles, the ten of pentacles, the ten of swords. A collection at maximum, like the moon at full; which moves from pentacles to swords, material to intellect and from earth to air.

This is a collection about orientation, finding a place: *the edge of the* (three times), *at the edge of* (three times), *in the centre of* (three times). The roots of freedom reach towards these coordinates.

This is a collection which knows drift: I make 91 poems of which only 16 are completed by a full stop or question mark. Sitting on a train a few days ago I watched the young skipping Tiktoks, always in motion, fingers bringing an ending before the end, and I thought of this collection.

This is an olefactory collection: *the smell of* (six times), a collection about desire: *I want to* (four times); also a relational collection: *and you are* (four times).

It is the collection of a photographer, which is to say it is a prism for viewing the world, and the collection of a collagist, as you see on the front cover. When I look at the front cover I want to see lambs (blessed is the lamb / did he who made the lamb make thee?) but when I look straight at it I'm not sure lambs were ever there at all.

This is a collection which knows Anne Carson (the phoenix mourns by shaping, weighing, testing, hollowing, plugging and carrying towards the light), Sylvia Plath, Dylan Thomas, Ocean Vuong, Richie Hofmann, Richard Siken, Clarice Lispector.

This is a collection which knows Kateryna Kalytko, who writes:

> The language broke at the folds
> and the shards sparkled like coal.

This is a collection which knows Ilya Kaminsky, who writes:

> Watch—
> Vasenka citizens do not know they are evidence of
>   happiness
>
> in a time of war,
>   each is a ripped-out document of laughter.

Ilya Kaminsky who writes: I chose English because no one in my family or friends knew it—no one I spoke to could read what I wrote.

I myself did not know the language. It was a parallel reality, an insanely beautiful freedom. It still is.

This is a collection that knows, with Deleuze and Guattari, the three characteristics of minor literature are the deterritorialization of language, the connection of the individual to a political immediacy, and the collective assemblage of enunciation. Real freedom is always controversial: in fact often we hate to be free—ask your analyst—we associate freedom with the psychoses. We associate psychoses-freedoms with fertility (the Bacchae: touch a wand to the ground and there comes a fountain of milk) and with trauma (Sarah Kane). It is controversial (free) perhaps for a free Ukrainian to free themselves to write poetry in English, or it is controversial (free) for English poetry to be freewritten by Ukrainian versification.

I like the way the collection nonchalantly drops into French now and then without warning: this makes me think of Michèle Lamy's music —or of her leaving a meeting at her own moment, without warning or excuse, like this collection.

Sláva Ukrayíni!

Nick Blackburn 24.11.22

Skin of Nocturnal Apple
© Misha Honcharenko

Cover artwork © Misha Honcharenko
Afterword © Nick Blackburn

Published in the U.K. by Pilot Press

First edition

Printed on 100% recycled paper

ISBN 978-1-7397029-2-2

Misha Honcharenko is a Ukrainian artist, photographer, poet and translator. He started his Instagram profile six years ago as a form of visual diary which since 24 February 2022 has been documenting his experiences of living in Ukraine during Russia's invasion.

Nick Blackburn is a psychoanalyst whose first book *The Reactor* was published by Faber in 2022. Nick is from North-West England and lives in London.